SETTLEMENT POEMS 1

BY
KRISTJANA GUNNARS

Turnstone Press gratefully acknowledges the support of the Multiculturalism Program, Government of Canada, which has aided in the publication of this book.

WINNIPEG: TURNSTONE PRESS, 1980

SETTLEMENT POEMS 1

Contents

Settlement Poems began after a visit with Prof. Sveinn Skorri Höskuldsson of the Department of Nordic Studies at the University of Iceland. His encouragement led to the research behind these poems. Historical sources were found in the National Library of Iceland in Reykjavik, where Olafur Hjartar kindly copied sections of the Library's holdings for me. Other historical sources were found at the Special Icelandic Collection of the Elizabeth Dafoe Library at the University of Manitoba, where Sigrid Johnson was kind enough to copy material for me as well. Acknowledgements are also due to Prof. Eli Mandel of the University of Toronto, who was writer-in-residence for Regina in 1978-79. His enthusiasm and kindness were helpful during the writing of the poems. Final thanks go to David Arnason of St. John's College at the University of Manitoba, whose encouraging response to Volume One was helpful in completing Volume Two.

— Kristjana Gunnars

FROM MEMORY I

(at most i've heard of 25
infants born to a woman
none of them twins
5 to 15 is average
2 to 4 might live

you expect them to die
you want them to die
food is scarce, life
is better where god is)

400 of us leave on the verona
wednesday july 12
from seydisfjördur, gudrídur   *history*
pregnant with a son
to cut trees in canada
                                      ⊣

(makes sure it's a son;
lay on her right side   *superstition*
during conception; pisses
into a washbasin under the moon   ·
puts a needle in the bottom

next morning: it's rusty, all's
well)
halldór briem interprets for us

son of eggert briem of skagafjördur
all the way to granton
july 16

(gudrídur is larger
on the right side, her right breast
is bigger: it's a boy)
for sure

leave granton by train
sunday to glascow, 4 days
later leave glascow at 12
thursday july 20

7

the trip goes well over the sea
the keel below is rusty
the east coast of canada grows
in the north, halldór briem

says it's virgin forest
all of it, says

they want more settlers
they call it
god's country

FROM MEMORY II

you want to know the trick of fertility
want to know the trick of infertility
to know how to stay together
know if the other is faithful

i'm forgetting fast
it's a long trip from glascow to quebec
this is the last story i'll tell

(hannes hannesson, scaleeye
turned 70 in 1885, told 3 stories
every night between february 2
& may 12 & still had more to tell)

the place is bottomless with stories
from glascow to quebec
you want to know about dusksleep days
when men lumbered in, threw off
their snowgear, put on the nightshoes
& sat down to knit, the women

sat down to knit too
(it's a long yarn) the best way

to stay together: don't air your quilt
on sundays, don't give each other
a sharp tool

eat the heart of a ptarmigan
put two tongues under your tongue & kiss
hang a raven's heart around your neck
hang a crow's heart around your neck

the best way
to test faithfulness: put
a magnet under her pillow at night
if she's true, she'll turn over & embrace you
if not, she'll turn over the other way
& fall with a crash on the floor
(or he will)

this is the last story i'll tell
the best way to become fertile: drink
mare's milk, dry a fox's testicle
in the shade, stir in wine, drink
after menstruation, or

(this is the only time i'll tell you)
during love, lie
with the hips above the shoulders
the best way

to avoid fertility: cut open your shin
put in a bit of mercury & heal over

there's more
i may tell you more, provided
you give me a long life in canada

FROM MEMORY III

gróa is dying
wife of jón ásmundsson from fáskrúdsfjördur
just before docking
july 31, she's made it to quebec

& gróa is dying
don't send me back
where the veinman bleeds me
bleeds me in fifty three places

puts the lancet in my navel
bleeds my eyebrows
till my eyeballs shrink & dry
bleeds my ear, bleeds with lancet

in my calf vein, my homecoming vein
gróa is dying
don't send me back

where the veinman sweats me
with a boil-up of vodka
tobacco, pepper, winds me
in eiderdown around my head

where the veinman ties me
to the bedpost while he works in the field
to sweat, collapse, wake again
sweat again, don't

send me back where the veinman
kneads an old woman like dough
down to an infant's size
wants to exchange us, exchange us

don't send me back
to be the veinman's changeling
don't
gróa is dying

just before docking

11

FROM MEMORY IV

an infant lies on gudrídur's belly
tied with umbilical cord
it lies in the grass
wails in the grass when the wind blows

birth on straw on the floor
birth on bearskin
birth in a winecellar

ólafur brynjólfsson meets us
in quebec monday july 31
helps halldór briem interpret
on the straw in a boxcar to toronto

he says don't listen
to the waiters in the winecellar
doorways on the quebec hills
who cry out to you: come in for a drink

he says don't eat with cracked spoon
or you'll have a harelip
don't step over a cat in heat
you'll be an idiot, don't look
at the northern lights, you'll be
cross-eyed, don't eat a ptarmigan's egg
the child will be crippled

the infant is born on bearskin in hay
a good sign
it won't feel the cold wind
that seeps through the sliding door
rattling across the quebec hills

FROM MEMORY V

leave quebec late at night
for montreal, 180 miles southwest
gulls & hawks circle
in the distancing east

the legs of the young ones
soft, pulpy with water
have to be opened to dry
the scales drop quickly, quickly

pelicans stand on stumps
at the shrinking pier, a heavy
vulture lands on a wagging branch

have to slit it down the length
of its back, under the toes
down to the last joint, have to
remove the tendons

have to write a daybook

arrive montreal midday
tuesday august 1, eat
the daymeal, walk in the brush
gather quills for a daybook

quills of young ducks, geese
still in the pin-feather age
quills full of water, blood
slow-drying, fly-blown

soft, have to slit them
soak the liquid up on paper
have to paint them outside
turn the pages heavy with them

have to write a daybook
with moist scaly quills
write a book of settlements
on the way to kingston

slow-drying, fly-blown

13

FROM MEMORY VI

treat me like a collection of eggs

don't kick the door down
don't scowl at the interpreter
halldór briem is blameless

in kingston, stepping off
the wagon for a nightmeal
with or without money
you can only go so far with milkteeth

somewhere they drop off
it's natural, have to sit down
with separated jaws
treat me like brittle china

when the restaurateur rolls out the tray
my skull rattles
especially the incisors
in the sudden shift of temperature

enamel shrinks faster than toothbone

give me paper to eat
so my teeth won't chip
especially the incisors

brittle as delicate china
don't kick the door down on me

FROM MEMORY VII

can't get used to the bugs

reach toronto wednesday
august 2, the bugs
accumulate in my armpits
on my neck, corners of my eyes

more & more of them
the further west i go
hungry, food supply still scarce
for them, feel them even
when i don't see them

work on my skull
bacon beetles or buffalo bugs
looking for new material
hard & dry from the ship

a few icelanders
settled toronto in 73 & 74
say the bugs come from a coyote
carcass, from the dried feet
of a cow, say

you hardly feel them
clean your skull in 48 hours
(if it's small), do it
with fine-barbed larvae

leave the bones intact
don't destroy delicate structures
teeth don't fall out, sutures
don't gape, they clean a bat
wing without messing any

of the digits, bugging can be
done in 24 hours (if your meat
is dry, if you're decaying
already) you hardly feel it

except in the membranes
of the nasal passages, in the bug-
house dust, sometimes
the skin breaks out

thursday august 3, 10
at night, leave toronto
for collingwood, the bugs
follow in patches on my shins

lay eggs in my nostrils, drown
the view of water, breed
in my eyes, color
the air black, i understand

when the bugs are finished
when i reach the west
my skull & bones will drown

in plains of white bleached
still delicate bones
where water evaporates
ships run aground

& bats collapse from the sky

FROM MEMORY VIII

4 days' sailing to duluth
from collingwood, the ship
crowded with swine, sheep

i sleep in the trough
where the animals feed
drink from a tank with a bat

that hangs till dusk
in a crevice over my head
(have to get rid of it

don't want it when it rains)
suspend a fly hook of tiny minnow
with a fine gut leader

stretch a wire over the watertank
when it comes to drink
gets knocked into the water

fish it out, suspend it
by the head from a tangled net
(we all have stomach cramps)

over the ship's floor
a little brown big-eared bat
with spread wings, dark

red, brown blotches inside
because of clotted blood, because
of broken wings on water

with bleating livestock, nausea
arrive duluth august 7, late
at night, the interpreter says

the states are full of bats
but that's superstition, they've
been mennonites since 1871

they're safe

FROM MEMORY IX

memorize the grub of the new
place, stay in duluth
till saturday august 12

4 days, find sustenance
(an earthworm is earth
in a worm, no good)

a snail; an ant from a rotten
log, by the hundreds
in an ant hill, boiled

with dandelion; beetle larvae
from a rotting stump
boiled with arrowhead; roasted

grasshoppers from the plains
where the train rides
tomorrow in thousands

good food if first you break
away the wings & legs
get dumped on the train

carted over minnesota, some
would settle here if they could
in the grass

FROM MEMORY X

late at night the train stops
no one knows where
we are, the desert is silent
we wait, listen

out there a baby screams
sweeps with a broom, nips
chews twigs in branches
a bear moans, a calf snorts

in the dawn, step out:
end of steel
everyone is gone, brushprints
trace through the dust

pebbly dragmarks ahead
into bushland, claw traces
up a treetrunk, small marks
of teeth in patches

where bark was, a young boy
picks twigs off the ground
walks out of the bush
halldór briem cries out

to him "where are we"
"fisher's landing" he says
fisher's landing, we're here
step around the freightcar

look at the tree
whiskbrooms on the branches
"porcupine" he says
& walks into the plain

no baby, no bear, no
cow, it's all porcupine
ahead

FROM MEMORY XI

ways of death at fisher's landing
are so remarkable
i never stiffen

in the beerparlor, lose
25 pounds sterling from
my pocket, discover my new state
next morning, even so

i'm relaxed after death, completely
uncontorted, feel no pain
15 to 20 minutes is all
it takes (with less time

i might have revived)
the simplest death i ever
experienced, a flash of the gunny
sack, flick into the warm water

immediately taken out again
never stiff in any position
no one notices
all my money at fisher's landing

remarkable

√ FROM MEMORY XII

i begin to think the country
from quebec to winnipeg is based
on the pitfall principle
simple (but effective) traps

a container in the ground
a shallow water basin, a dis-
assembled box weighted
down with rock

an artificial fly, when i leap
the earth turns to water
a barrel sinks in the lake
raw meat lies on a ramp

wherever i look, spikes
stand ready to drive in
to my head, clip off my hand

a trench splits the road
especially on rainy nights
everything fills with water

unnecessary graveyards, all
the children complain about them
severe stomach pain
suffocation, insects in the mouth

3 days, august 14 to 17
on the steamboat to winnipeg
the drinking water is pure
poison by now, full

of creatures fallen in

FROM MEMORY XIII

reach winnipeg in the morning
august 17
the lake is in my head
the river is in my head
the flies are in my head

halldór briem keeps us
from stepping ashore, discusses
medicine with fridjón fridriksson

(soak my head in vinegar
spread the strong smell
of cloven nettleroot in the air

chop grassflower root, boil
thymeseed, give me hot footbath
cold footbath, let me sleep
with bare feet)

my head is soaking
(comb my hair with the horn
of a live sheep, steep
roseroot seed in my nose)

briem discusses
(wash my head with lye
with the ashes of a raven's head)
sail me backwards from winnipeg
let me go home (let me pin

a virgin's garter round my head)
all the old remedies

discuss them now

JÓHANN BRIEM I

i know about parasites
when piles of corpses are dumped
together they look for fresh

fields right away
after the host's death, you can
shake the animal & they tumble

out like sawdust, you can put
them in a sack, carry them
with you to the new place

this w.c. krieger, even sigtryggur
jónasson from canada, find
our fare inhospitable, good spring

lumpsucker & groats porridge
a full tureen of sour whey, they say
it's better west of the ocean

that the trade ban has ruined
our chances here: they don't find
fish stomachs, heads with liver

nutritious, iceland moss porridge
keeps you alive even
if you don't like to look

i wouldn't be too sure
we won't bring round worms
in our throats, crop, stomachs

intestines to canada, hell
they don't care with their
commission to sell, everyone

's going this summer, 76
twelve hundred in three lots
with steamship from saudárkrókur

25

friday june 30, 740 in all
from akureyri sunday july 2
752 people: this krieger

is gutting us, stomachs
livers, he's emptying the sack
of flesh as if we had

enough to lose, as if he had
enough to sell, large plots
in the west where he wants

to dump us, half dead

JÓHANN BRIEM II

the steamship verona reaches
⟋ granton on thursday july 6
& heads straight to glascow

we've begun to rehearse how
to see in darkness, to see
that which is hidden, to win
the love of strangers, to understand

the speech of birds, the foreign
tongues

on tuesday july 11 the allanline's
austria leaves for quebec

we've left our books in múlasýsla
to be burned, this will be
from memory, even bólu-einar
andrésson's books were burned

in 1885, there are over 700
of us to learn the methods
from memory: how to see

by night; smear the blood
of a mouse, the belly of a white
rabbit, the eyeball of an eagle
around your eyes: how to see

hidden things; how to succeed;
dry a raven's head in the wind
where no sun shines & a white
black stone drops from the brain

wind the stone in unused flax
& carry it under your left armpit:
how to win love; dry
a pigeon's heart & hang it

round your neck, all will love you

on the st. lawrence river, ólafur
brynjélfsson from bólsstadarhlíd
brings a letter signed by ten
icelanders in nova scotia:

don't settle nova scotia
by any means, not here: how
to learn the speech of birds;

wash a merlin's tongue, bury it
in honey, smear on the membrane
of a wagtail's brain & keep

that tongue under your tongue
for three nights in a row:
the birds will talk, the birds
of the forest will speak

JÓHANN BRIEM III

don't have to worry

leave quebec sunday july 23
by railroad
& the runes of the line
begin to draw on the west

if you're prepared: who cares
draw three wreaths
of karlamagnús, seal of david
seal of solomon, seal
of king ólafur on the chest
draw it in blood
with the feather of a water-rail

leave toronto july 27
by rail to collingwood, sarnia

draw it on the fingernails
of the sick, draw it on a slice
of bread for a thief
to eat, it's all right

leave sarnia july 28
by steamboat across lake huron
lake superior to duluth, tuesday
night, august 1

to escape the power of the runes:
carry salt, carry flour, carry
steel in a linen bag
& if none of this works

if the train reaches fisher's
landing august 4
& nothing still works out

it's all right, all
you have to do when you step out
in the morning
is to suck some piss up your nose

JÓHANN BRIEM IV

the finest wizard of the north

saemundur fródi says
there are other ways
to escape a sense of evil
on a wicked journey

by steamship north
on red river august 5
two large flatboats like eyes
one tied on each side
of the steamer, looking east
looking west, arriving

in winnipeg tuesday august 8
six o clock at night

where a human brain is buried
in thought of winter
& memory is three months long
towards the north

to flee the man
who doesn't want you, don't
recite the our
father forwards & backwards

saemundur fródi says
there are other ways
soak a stolen brass
in your own blood

pull an eye
pull a man's head
out of your own blood

steal an imp
of a man's rib
from a grave at whitsun

galdra-leifi, another wizard
watered a man's head
with wine & bread
& with it he read the future

what they'll pull from your blood
once you're dead

but death isn't necessary
saemundur fródi says

there are other ways

to journey the north

JÓHANN BRIEM V

in most ways i'm human

except
the septum of my nose is missing
my upper lip bulges
where humans have a rift

in other ways i'm normal
except
i'm invisible
when i don't want to be seen

marry me, you disappear
i marry you, it's ok
weaving, fishing, raking
i can do all that

waited 5 conspicuous
days in winnipeg, at 3
august 13 we disappear again
on 6 boxes up red river

wasn't so bad, i'm normal
lie with humans
in crags & knolls, grateful
for a good deed

on the first day
the little rowboats don't get far
cross selkirk august 16
reach lake winnipeg august 17
reach gimli august 20, sunday

invisible people
otherwise friendly, except
when it's a broken promise
like a broken bridge

where one side won't connect
with the other, my way
is to switch infants
i'm good at that, switching

human infants around

you won't know the difference

JÓHANN BRIEM VI

it's a lot of luggage
i'm taking to the grave

the flatboats won't cross
all the rest of august
i'm carting trunks over

lake winnipeg, back & back
again from the rivermouth
to gimli, it's a dream

i'm settling, a little cemetery

i intend to fill
when winter closes in, plugs
the breathing holes with caked mud

i'll begin to rot, rot
complete, entire, flesh
hair, nails, bones, & you

when you discover my grave
later, much later, in spring
dig up my skull

my eyes will move
in your hands, then
you can call yourself three times

see yourself row across the lake
dreamperson
to tell you what you want to know

STEFÁN EYJÓLFSSON I

when i was in reykjavík
from 70-74, eyjólfur talked
about moving out, making
a clean kill

in brazil or canada
& when we arrived he changed
his mind, wounded i think
watching the caribou kill

even though it was clean
no slow throat-cut death
i was careful, crept
grasped the antlers, he

couldn't move, his head
forced down gave me a clean neck
& i thrust the narrow-tipped
skinning knife in just back

of the bone-ridge by the brain
into the spinal cord & eyjólfur
tore up like brushfire
berserk, yelled

we don't need the caribou, ah
but he's too late, the animal
died in an instant
without blood, without bowels

STEFÁN EYJÓLFSSON II

jón taylor, the man who made us
trail to settle lake winnipeg
now tells us to go back
like flying squirrels, settle

here, fly, tree to tree
doubtless he's flustered, didn't
expect to lead us to death

no, after ontario with no
space in winnipeg we'll go
on, back in the dakotas

saw a flying squirrel hole
in a fir, a hickory nut opened
with holes in the side
never believed in flying mammals

till the fir exploded, soaring
squirrels flashed off
shadows above in the trees
ticking into the trunks, hell

anything's possible, even if
less than two hundred of us
journey north tomorrow

when the squirrel lands
with a muffled thud in the snow
four pawprints & a crunch of fur
it, too, drags forward

STEFÁN EYJÓLFSSON III

we're ready
the square flat-bottomed boats
nestle east of notre dame street
with our trunks, tools
the captains count before we board

jón taylor stands on the bank
seems dark up north
where the red river current goes
tell him so, "it's dimming"

taylor's quiet for a while
then says i can stay behind
it's the future, not the sky i saw
but let him stay flatfooted

against a clod of mud
a whitetail jackrabbit snuggles
ready to speed away any
given moment
on hind legs, further down

by the water the poet crouches
with a drying board, presses
steel pins round the edges
for drying rabbit skins
up north, white skins

rubbed grey with hardwood ashes
he too looks up the red river
where the first flatboat floats
with the current, looks north
into time

STEFÁN EYJÓLFSSON IV

the first boat sails
oars spread in all directions
both rudders, fore & aft, tighten

the poet's hareskin is cased

brittle-dry with a split
head, wide cheeks, thin nose
"a difficult filling," the poet
crumples paper

winds tight oakum around
for the new head
"idiot filling" he calls it
when i approach, the first
flatboat headed for the deep

brittle time of stone
"hope we don't all run aground"

the hare's legs
wound with tow, spliced
with sticks, filled with cotton
even the ears are scrubbed
free of cartilage

the fur pinned on his board

he looks north again, decides
to pin down the ears
during freight, says
"when it's dry, when

we get to new iceland
we'll remove the cotton & spread it flat"

STEFÁN EYJÓLFSSON V

keels pass with the current
one night, one day
everett parson at the helm

the poet tries to fish
lops the handle off a spoon
pins a hook on, flings it

into his own arm
the wound appears thin
punctures deep

behind us they're stranded on sand
& we wait at the shore
one after another

the boats run into stones
next day, sunday
taylor holds service, the poet

shakes, says he didn't bleed
himself enough yesterday
after the wound, two days

later, weakened
he whispers the hook remained
in the arm, the flesh
swells round, red

lake winnipeg at the end
of red river, says
what he wanted was

a separate life

STEFÁN EYJÓLFSSON VI

the poet can't preserve his skin
can't clean it on the crowded flatboat

it's a goose off the water
he skins, washes blood stains
out of feathers, leaves the fat

the skin is riddled with fat, the poet

rubs fine salt on the inside
into the skull, at the bill
& folds it lengthwise

the flesh sides touch, salted

taylor is sore
this is his idea
reserving the lakeside
for new iceland

bringing us into an empty stomach
without the cattle, hay that lured us

but he doesn't speak
doesn't need to be reminded

our mid-october plains camp
will have to do

ólafur ólafsson from espihóll
sits nearest the lean-to
with burrowing eyes, he's seen

the track, front paw big, back
paw small, belongs to a wolf
seen where it's scratched

maybe for ruffed grouse, but there's
no blood on the new snow
yet, it'll come he thinks

too, after duluth it's been hard
after the last rail station

on the rivers, arriving here
after a promise of hay, cows:
nothing

there's the plaintive prairie
wolf night-call again
long clear melancholic call

breaks into a yap, ólafur
who led us to winnipeg
scours the fresh snow with his hand

without cows, milk, how long
is it possible to scratch out
an existence

with no preparation, empty
promise of snow-furrow
where grouseblood is

missing, yes
the coyote's been here
with a high-pitched wail

just ahead of us

STEFÁN EYJÓLFSSON VIII

still waiting for the three
commissioned by the government
to bring cows, can't live
without milk

been down the western
slope of lake winnipeg
along a brush wolf trail

the place sigtryggur jónasson wrote
is dotted with game, fish
good for a scattering of us
from milwaukee, the trail

through the brush has signposts
rocks, tufts, stumps
full of wolf or coyote scats

found one large & heavy
with hair like a little cow
especially at intersections
where trail meets trail

found knolls of them
coyote scats, learn to read them
fast, half liquid after meat
crumbly after pine nuts & chokecherry

coyote scats, settlement runes

STEFÁN EYJÓLFSSON IX

it's cooling, by the time
i've split these planks the lake
will be frozen, i won't fish

ice-seines tighten over
the rushes, grasses, barkslabs
i've woven into the walls
& the roof i've slanted back
to reflect the fire

ice seines cling to the sapling
boughs i've driven
into the ground: to hold us down
in storm, to keep our own weight

up, cling in the aspen fingers
intertwined for support

november begins, blizzard
gameless, snowed-over access
magnús thinks we'll get frozen

milk, meat from neighbors
no, the packs of snow pull us in
it's hard enough to keep

my own body up, own heat in
when november opens the door
it closes, weaves up the sky
with iceglaze boughs

STEFÁN EYJÓLFSSON X

catch 37

flat-sided pike in the red
river shallow up for dawn
feeding, taylor tells me
to give it to those run

out of food, some have nothing

can't take fishing the shelter-
less red river
bring them in to gimli
after the morning to gut
them, their stomachs empty

after the night's digestion
taylor tells me where the need is
greatest, empties his pocket
of coins, says he's tried to move

food out but it's going
poorly, some have nothing & then

we fill the little chests
with hungry pike, drench them
with white wood chips, one

for each hollow family, one
for me

STEFÁN EYJÓLFSSON XI

it's the rabbit that keeps us
in life, the white one
the split-lipped one
the one with twins, set

a snare in the runway
against a stump, a small loop
of fishline, a sapling tied
into a broken tree

i think we've split, some
who stayed in winnipeg, didn't
come north, don't
burden themselves with us now

memory is short
the rabbit's caught up
off the ground, flying hard
when i arrive to skin it

to take life for life, cut
round the middle, pull
the fur off, chop
the head & feet off with

a hunting knife, cut from throat
to tail through the pelvic bone
rib cage, around the genitals
pull the organs through the pelvic

opening, wash away the blood

of the past, take life
stuff the inside with fresh
sapling boughs & carry it, the rabbit
home, life for life on my back

STEFÁN EYJÓLFSSON XII

it's not a blank book
just another language, this map
of well-defined patches

open the cut at the breast bone
back to the vent
through the abdomen, slip
the edge of the scalpel under

the skin, wall opens with a shot
of knife, intestine juices run
sprinkle sawdust on the flesh
to catch, dry, poke out

the knee joint, cut tendons
separate bones, run
my thumbnail behind the meat
& the skin rips down the side

hook up the little map
by the hips, slice out
the stomach: mammal teeth
claws, hair, feathers, feet

chewed by no bill's teeth

this stomach reads well
defines
the sustenance of a new land

STEFÁN EYJÓLFSSON XIII

when air turns to ice crystal
it won't breathe well
turns to a mirror
reflects mirages: keep seeing
cows with milk
bulging warm & fat
the tracks are clear in snow

a wallow where the cow grazed
a trunk worn smooth
where it rubbed, see the long
kinky brown hair clinging

but magnús says this cow
has a hump, tears up the spring
ground with horns
when it's soggy, rolls
the hunchbacked body caked
in mud, might have been

our cattle, oxen, hay

but this is bison, magnús
says migrated away
& the tracks they've left us

look like shadows
of lungs, small, fading
lungs in the snow
through where the crystal
ogees blow

STEFÁN EYJÓLFSSON XIV

i'm down to collecting skeletons
bones with deeper relations
than flesh or skin, bones that show
how we live, seven

are dead at fridjón's, two
left, at ólafur's the third
baby swells in the gums
blood streaks the white teeth

scurvy cuts away the flesh
as cleanly as it can, removes
the skin, viscera, bones
too small, too delicate

to be touched hang together
by thin ligaments, tags
of leather separate the segments
the hatchets of disease do

rough work among us
cut the tendons that join
cheek bones, pelvic bones, deep
bones loosen like ribs

i'm buckling under, can't watch
ólafur's third one bruise, swell
thirty five are dead, every
third one of us, a child

a weak adult, the saw
of scurvy picks away
the eyes, scrapes the brain
out of the skull, washes out

the loosened brain, folds
the legs, limbs, ties up
the marrowed bones in rags
bones, deep bleeding bones, see

how we hang in the sun to dry

STEFÁN EYJÓLFSSON XV

i've jotted my notes in the corner
of the newsprint sigtryggur
brought from reykjavík, paper
soiled now with offal

our first battle, first winter
is past: every third man
rolled up, burned or buried
it's a long trip we're taking

we bleed freely like freshly
killed birds, now we lie
for a short time, coagulate
the blood on our feathers

i've learned to leave it at that
the bird, to plug the throat
with a ball of oilcloth, put
wads of string in the nostrils

when the blood continues to creep
out, the bird stiffens
very fast, a tap with the hammer
snaps the wingbones in two

once settled, on our backs
like this we can't fly again
we're mounted into the prairie
pinned by broken promise, by

confusion, each man thinks
for himself now, the feathers parted
with a barren strip, pinned
by the unwilling in winnipeg

who won't make the journey north
with food, our own people
cut off
in the middle of the breast

STEFÁN EYJÓLFSSON XVI

our other side
builds this settlement
the side with a drillhole

where the fluid seeps out
through the tip of the wind's
blowpipe, the side out of which

pressed air is forced
the way you learn to blow eggs
however incubated

the careful work
with forceps & scissors, how
to pull it out piecemeal

hairs, feathers, the way
you learn to digest it, mouth
by mouth, to drain the shell

yes, the other side
of blowing eggs with chicks
inside is messy work

messy work, but you learn how
to be born
piecemeal

Kristjana Gunnars was born in Reykjavik, Iceland, in 1948. She immigrated to Canada in 1969, after doing undergraduate work in Oregon. She has lived in rural British Columbia, Vancouver, Toronto, Winnipeg, and Regina, where she took an M.A. in literature. Gunnars worked as a schoolteacher in rural Iceland in 1973-74, and taught English at the University of Regina from 1976-78. She is now researching the history and literature of Icelandic settlers in Canada. Her poems have appeared in various journals in Canada and the U.S.

Turnstone Press
Settlement Poems 1
by Kristjana Gunnars

This book was designed by Gudrun
Rohatgi. The map reproduced on the cover
is by Professor Gissur Eliasson. The
photograph of Halldór Briem is from *The
Icelandic Canadian*, Summer, 1975.

Turnstone Press
St. John's College
University of Manitoba
Winnipeg, Manitoba
R3T 2M5

Previous Publications from Turnstone Press:

In the Gutting Shed by W.D. Valgardson
Open Country by George Amabile
the lands I am by Patrick Friesen
Changehouse by Michael Tregebov
Seems Valuable by Ed Upward
Seed Catalogue by Robert Kroetsch
The Inside Animal by Arthur Adamson
Blowing Dust off the Lens by Jim Wallace
bluebottle by Patrick Friesen
Soviet Poems by Ralph Gustafson
Rehearsal for Dancers by Craig Powell
Mister Never by Miriam Waddington
The Cranberry Tree by Enid Delgatty Rutland
Rock Painter by R.E. Rashley
First Ghost to Canada by Kenneth McRobbie
No Longer Two People by Pat Lane and Lorna Uher
The Earth Is One Body by David Waltner-Toews
The Man with the Styrofoam Head by Gregory Grace
When the Dogs Bark at Night by Valerie Reed
The Bridge, That Summer by A.E. Ammeter
This Body That I Live In by Anne Le Dressay
Mother's Gone Fishing by Norma Dillon
Almost a Ritual by Les Siemieniuk
Jimmy Bang Poems by Victor Enns
Across the White Lawn by Robert Foster
Shore Lines by Douglas Barbour
Interstices of Night by Terrence Heath
No Country for White Men by Gordon Turner
Scarecrow by Douglas Smith
A Planet Mostly Sea by Tom Wayman

Date

5 200